SCHOLASTIC INC.

New York   Toronto   London   Auckland   Sydney

Exclusive worldwide licensing agent: Momentum Partners, Inc., New York, NY
Photo credits:

front cover: (bat) K.W. Fink/Ardea London Ltd.; (sloth) Gerry Ellis/ENP; (Kratts) 1998 Paragon Entertainment Corporation **back cover**: (giraffe) Zig Leszczynski/Animals Animals; (Kratts) 1998 Paragon Entertainment Corporation; (frilled lizard) Klaus Uhlenhut/Animals Animals

p. 4: Laura Wilkinson/1998 Paragon Entertainment Corporation; **p. 5**: Anthony Bannister/1998 Paragon Entertainment Corporation; **p. 6**: Laura Wilkinson/1998 Paragon Entertainment Corporation; **p. 7**: Jeremy Stafford-Deitsch/ENP; **p. 8**: Fred Bavendam/Peter Arnold, Inc; **p. 9**: Mark Stouffer/Animals Animals; **p. 10**: (top) M. Reardon/Photo Researchers, Inc.; (bottom) 1998 Paragon Entertainment Corporation; **p. 11**: M. Edwards/Still Pictures/Peter Arnold, Inc.; (inset) Laura Wilkinson/1998 Paragon Entertainment Corporation; **p. 12**: Martin Wendler/NHPA; **p. 13**: Roland Seitre/Peter Arnold, Inc.; **p. 14**: Daniel Heuclin/NHPA; **p. 15**: Fred McConnaughey/Photo Researchers, Inc.; **p. 16**: David C. Fritts/Animals Animals; **p. 17**: Bruce Davidson/Animals Animals; **p. 18**: Dianne Blell/Peter Arnold, Inc.; **p. 19**: (top left and right) Anthony Bannister/1998 Paragon Entertainment Corporation; (bottom right) Fritz Prenzel/Tony Stone Images; (bottom left) Ed Reschke/Peter Arnold, Inc.; **p. 20**: (top) J.H. Robinson/Animals Animals; (bottom) Richard Goss/OSF/Animals Animals; **p. 21**: (top) H.C. Kappel/BBC/ENP; (bottom) Tom McHugh/Photo Researchers, Inc.; **p. 22**: (top) Laura Wilkinson/1998 Paragon Entertainment Corporation; (bottom) Norbert Wu/Tony Stone Images, Inc.; **p. 23**: (top) Michael Dick/Animals Animals; (bottom) Keith Gillett/Animals Animals; **p. 24**: (top) Johnny Johnson/Animals Animals; (bottom) Franz Gorski/Peter Arnold, Inc.; **p. 25**: (all) Anthony Bannister/1998 Paragon Entertainment Corporation; **p. 26**: Gerard Lacz/Animals Animals; **p. 27**: (top) Michael Dick/Animals Animals; (bottom) Leonard Lee Rue III/Photo Researchers, Inc.; **p. 28**: (top) Bob and Clara Calhoun/Bruce Coleman Inc.; (bottom) Anthony Mercieca/ Photo Researchers, Inc.; (inset) Laura Wilkinson/1998 Paragon Entertainment Corporation; **p. 29**: (top) Donald Specker/Animals Animals; (bottom) Zig Zeszczynski/Animals Animals; **p. 30**: (Kratts) Laura Wilkinson/1998 Paragon Entertainment Corporation; (bat) K.W. Fink/Ardea London Ltd.; **p. 31**: (top) Gerry Ellis/ENP; (bottom) Steven David Miller/Animals Animals; **p. 32**: (top) Morten Strange/NHPA; (bottom) Peter Ward/Bruce Coleman Inc.; **p. 33**: Andrew J. Martinez/Photo Researchers, Inc.; **p. 34**: Anthony Bannister/1998 Paragon Entertainment Corporation; **p. 35**: Tom Brakefield/Bruce Coleman Inc.; **p. 36**: Fritz Polking/Peter Arnold, Inc.; **p. 37**: Howard Hall/OSF/Animals Animals; **p. 38**: (top) M. Reardon/Photo Researchers, Inc.; (bottom) Laura Wilkinson/1998 Paragon Entertainment Corporation; **p. 39**: (top) K.G. Vock/Okpia/Photo Researchers, Inc.; (bottom) Roland Seitre/Peter Arnold, Inc.; **p. 40**: (all) Laura Wilkinson/1998 Paragon Entertainment Corporation; **p. 41**: (top left and right) Fred McConnaughey/Photo Researchers, Inc.; (bottom left) Stephen J. Krasemann/DRK Photo; (bottom right) S. J. Krasemann/Peter Arnold, Inc.; **p. 42**: (top left) Zig Leszczynski/Animals Animals; (top right) Michael Fogden/Animals Animals; (bottom left) Michael Dick/Animals Animals; (bottom right) Klaus Uhlenhut/Animals Animals; **p. 43**: Bertram G. Murray, Jr./Animals Animals; **p. 44**: Anthony Bannister/1998 Paragon Entertainment Corporation; **p. 45**: Norbert Wu/Tony Stone Images, Inc.; **p. 46**: Roland Seitre/Peter Arnold, Inc; **p. 47**: (top) Roland Seitre/Peter Arnold, Inc.; (bottom) Adrienne T. Gibson/ Animals Animals; **p. 48**: Laura Wilkinson/1998 Paragon Entertainment Corporation

ISBN 0-590-53741-5

Copyright © 1998 by Paragon Entertainment Corporation.
All rights reserved. Published by Scholastic Inc.

Book design by Todd Lefelt

12 11 10 9 8 7 6 5 4 3 2 1   8 9/9 0 1 2 3/0

Printed in the U.S.A.
First Scholastic printing, January 1998

A Wild Welcome From Martin and Chris

Scientists have discovered more than 1,000,000 kinds of insects, over 21,000 types of fish, nearly 9,000 kinds of birds, around 6,500 kinds of reptiles, more than 4,500 different mammals, and about 4,000 varieties of amphibians!

Okay, gang, get ready for some incredible animal facts. They just may make your brain bubble with amazement.

The Buddy System

Most little creatures steer clear of larger, more dangerous animals. After all, they don't want to become somebody's lunch.

But sometimes you'll find unusual animal partners who live close together and help each other survive.

Moray eel

Cleaner wrasse

When the cleaner wrasse wants a tasty meal, she swims inside the jaws of a moray eel and chows down on parasites and diseased skin. The eel doesn't mind because, hey, if *you* had parasites and diseased skin in *your* mouth, wouldn't *you* want someone to get rid of them?!

The poisonous tentacles of the sea anemone zap most fish to death. But the brightly colored clownfish can safely swim among the tentacles without getting hurt at all. In fact, when the clownfish is hungry, she eats particles of leftover fish that are stuck to the sea anemone's tentacles. This keeps the sea anemone clean and the clownfish full. The clownfish also chases away the sea anemone's enemies, such as butterfly fish. At night, the clownfish gets protection by sleeping on top of the sea anemone's tentacles.

Clown fish

Sea anemone

Sand tiger shark

Remora

The remora fish, nicknamed the "sharksucker," has a wild way of traveling through the ocean — he hitches a ride with various sharks. A remora uses the flat, oval sucker on the top of his head to attach himself to the top or underside of a shark's body. This way, remoras are protected by their bigger buddy and get food scraps that fall from the shark's mouth. Remoras are lucky that sharks eat other kinds of fish and don't seem to mind the extra company.

Even though he is the second-largest mammal on land and has very few natural enemies, the rhinoceros keeps on the lookout for danger! But they don't have great vision so it is hard for them to see when an enemy approaches. Luckily for the rhino, the red-billed oxpecker acts as a kind of "watch bird." The oxpecker, who eats insects from the rhino's back, calls out if she sees another animal approaching.

By sticking together, the rhino gets a cleaner skin and the oxpecker gets an all-she-can-eat bug banquet.

As Big As They Come

Make way for some extra-large animals. We're talking the largest lizard, the most colossal clam, the biggest bear, the most whopping whale, and more. These creatures spend most of their time searching for food to fuel their giant bodies. If any of these maxi-monsters seem to be looking at you hungrily, just remind yourself, "It's only a book . . . it's only a book."

Blue whale

This is how big I am compared to the blue whale.

Meet the awesome, drop-your-jaw-in-disbelief blue whale. She's the largest animal in the world! This massive mammal is 100 feet long and weighs a titanic 150 tons. Try fitting one of *these* on your bathroom scale! If you lined up three blue whales from head to tail, they would be as long as a football field. When it comes to stuffing their faces, blue whales go for plankton and krill, which are small creatures that float in the ocean. And talk about all-you-can-eat: These whales have been known to eat two tons of these tiny creatures in a single meal.

The anaconda is a mighty constrictor that lives in South America. He can grow to be over 25 feet long — as wide as a tennis court — and is the world's heaviest snake — sometimes tipping the scales at 600 pounds. Anacondas have been known to eat a whole deer in a single, very long gulp. To swallow an animal that's much larger than his head, this snake has to unhinge his jaw. After a meal like that, he won't have to eat again for another month.

Komodo dragon

Leaping lizards! This massive, powerful reptile known as the Komodo dragon can grow to be 11 feet long and weigh 350 lbs. That's as heavy as two refrigerators! She lives in Indonesia, on the island of Komodo, and although she can't breathe fire, this "dragon" (actually a type of monitor lizard) can kill and eat very large prey such as water buffalo. But they're not picky. If there aren't any living animals around, Komodo dragons are happy to munch on carrion (dead, decaying creatures). Yuck!

Goliath frog

The goliath frog of West Africa is over 12 inches long and weighs over 7 pounds! Just two goliath frogs are as heavy as a bowling ball. Because he weighs so much, he can't jump very high (even during leap years!). Instead, he hides in the marshes and wetlands, and waits for his favorite prey to come to him — fish, snakes, insects, and other frogs. The goliath frog's enormous Ping-Pong-ball eyes not only help him spot meals, they also help him gulp down his food. When a goliath frog swallows, he closes his eyes, which makes his eyeballs push down against the roof of his mouth. That pushes the unlucky victim down his throat.

Giant clam

This super shellfish can be found in the Great Barrier Reef off Australia and in shallow waters of the Indian and Pacific oceans. She's about 4 feet long and weighs over 550 pounds. The giant clam's shell gets lots of sunlight, making her shell the ideal home for the colorful algae that live on the outside of her body. While most types of clams use a special footlike organ to move around on the ocean floor, the giant clam stays put most of the time.

Perhaps the biggest bear of them all is the Kodiak, also known as the Alaskan brown bear. Fully grown, this impressive creature weighs 1,000 pounds — about as heavy as a concert grand piano! This bear eats fish, small animals, roots, berries, and other plants. Female Kodiak bears become fierce fighters if they need to defend their young.

Kodiak bear

Goliath beetle

The goliath beetle weighs as much as a baseball, which is a lot for a bug! He lives in the tropical rain forests in Africa, where his favorite meal is — **Yeeech!** — rotten fruit. To breathe, the goliath beetle inhales and exhales through tiny tubes located on his belly.

African elephants

At birth, an African elephant already weighs about 250 pounds. By the time a male elephant is fully grown, he weighs 16,500 pounds — about as much as the tractor that pulls an 18-wheeler! He stands 13 feet high and measures 25 feet long from trunk to tail. Adult elephants use their impressive trunks to eat over 200 pounds of plants a day.

Long-Lost Cousins?

Rhinoceros

Elephant

Kangaroo

Lion

Wait a second! This section isn't about rhinos, lions, elephants, or kangaroos! We're talking about rhinoceros *beetles*, *ant* lions, elephant *shrews*, and kangaroo *rats*. While these wacky creatures aren't really related to their bigger namesakes, in some ways they sure do share a kooky resemblance. See how these animals rely on their basic physical features to help them survive.

Ant lion

Ant

Roooaaarrr!! Those mighty jaws belong to the ant lion — a small insect that is not an ant or a lion. To catch unsuspecting ants in sandy areas, this creature creates sand traps. First, she uses her head as a shovel to create deep holes in the sand. Then, the ant lion hides at the bottom of her trap. When her prey walks on the trap, it caves in and the unlucky ant falls downward — straight into the jaws of the ant lion. If a sneaky ant tries to walk away from the trap, the ant lion will often whip sand at the ant until it slides down into her pit of death. Then the ant lion grabs the ant and eats it.

Elephant shrew

The elephant shrew, found in Africa, has a long, narrow, floppy snout that helps him find and eat ants, termites, and beetles. His snout looks a bit like the great elephant creature feature, the trunk. The elephant shrew usually travels on all fours, but when he's surprised, he'll sometimes hop around on his back legs with his tail in the air, looking like a rubber ball.

Rhinoceros beetle

When male rhinoceros beetles fight with each other, the stronger beetle will sometimes use his horn to pick up the weaker one and drop him somewhere else. When it comes to heavy lifting, the rhino beetle is incredibly strong. If necessary, this mighty creature can support 850 times his weight on his back.

Kangaroo rat

Although the kangaroo rat doesn't have a pouch, her large hind legs remind many people of the Australian kangaroo. This rodent's legs are not only terrific for scurrying and hopping across the desert, they also help the kangaroo rat to communicate with others. At night, this animal will quickly tap her feet near the underground homes of family members. Scientists believe that these stomps help warn her desert neighbors about nearby danger or they can even give information about herself, such as her age and gender. Young adult male kangaroo rats usually drum their feet the fastest. To get water in the dry desert, kangaroo rats bury seeds deep underground until the seeds absorb moisture from the soil. Then they eat the seeds.

May We Have The Envelope, Please?

Welcome to the Kratt **MBP** Award Ceremony. Those initials stand for **Most Bizarre Part**. To be eligible for this honor, an animal must have a unique creature feature, a body part that is simply extraordinary. And the winners are . . .

squid eye

The largest eyeball in the world belongs to an enormous underwater creature, the giant squid. Her eye is about 16 inches across. That's about as wide as the open book you're holding in your hands.

For the proboscis monkey, everything's coming up noses! Male proboscis monkeys use their super schnozzolas to attract female proboscis monkeys, who find an oversized nose irresistible.

Proboscis monkey

Coconut crab

If the coconut crab didn't have such super strong claws, she wouldn't be able to get her favorite food — pizza! No, just kidding. This crab is nuts about coconuts. When this tropical creature gets hungry, she climbs a tall coconut tree and cracks open the hard shells to get at the sweet, white fruit inside.

African elephant

Without a doubt, the animal with the largest ears and the biggest nose is the male African elephant. His enormous ears — which can grow as huge as four feet across — are able to pick up low frequency sounds that humans can't hear. These massive ears also prevent him from overheating. As warm blood travels near the thin skin on the underside of his ears, it is cooled. The cooler blood then circulates and cools the rest of the body. His nose, usually called a trunk, contains over 30,000 muscles and tendons.

Dogs, as you probably know, have an amazing sense of smell. This German shepherd, for example, has a million times more smelling power than humans. The secret is that the inside of his nose contains over 40 times the number of smell-cells we have.

German shepherd

Even though a giraffe's neck is longer than most people's entire body, it only contains seven bones. In fact, that's the same number of bones as in a human neck. The big difference is that a giraffe's neck bones are each about 10 inches long. To pump blood up his long neck, a giraffe has a humongous heart that weighs 25 pounds, is 2 feet long, and has walls that are up to 3 inches thick.

Giraffes

The giraffe also wins an MBP award for his 18-inch tongue, which comes in handy for carefully pulling leaves from thorn-covered acacia trees.

Okapi

Another African creature with an amazing tongue is the okapi. Although an adult okapi is much shorter than a giraffe (less than five feet from her shoulders to the ground), her talented tongue is so long, she can use it to lick her eyes.

Tapir

The tapir has phenomenal feet, with tremendous toes. Each of his feet has three large, flexible toes. Both of his back feet also have an additional small toe. When a tapir puts his foot down on the muddy ground, his large toes spread apart and then go together again as he lifts his foot. This allows him to easily zip through the muddy swamps and forests of Central America. And his toe power doesn't stop there! When he pulls his flexible toes together, they can form a thin point, allowing the tapir to easily slide out of the muddy ground.

Spider monkey

Although the South American spider monkey can't spin a web, she has one of the most talented tails in the world. She can grab things just like a hand can. In fact, the spider monkey's tail is so strong and flexible that she spends much of her life hanging upside down from tree limbs. She can even use her tail to pick up small objects off the ground.

The hummingbird gets his name because he can beat his wings so fast — up to 80 times per second — that he creates a humming sound as he flies. The hummingbird is an acrobatic flyer that can go straight up like a helicopter, backwards, and even upside down. That's what you call a real twirly bird!

To get enough nectar to fuel all this flying, this high-energy creature may visit 2,000 flowers a day. Some people think hummingbirds never stop flying and don't have legs. But that's not true, see?

If you woke up one morning and found out you had 100 legs, you'd probably freak out. Not only that, you'd have a really tough time walking to the bathroom without tripping over yourself. But if you were a millipede, an insect that has up to *200* legs, walking with all those legs would be a piece of cake. The millipede's body has a complicated network of nerves that automatically sends messages to and from her brain to help control all of those limbs.

Millipede

Basket starfish

Okay, okay, that waking up with 100 legs idea was pretty strange. But what if you woke up and saw you had 50 arms? That's what a basket starfish does every morning. If you ever meet a basket starfish, you can greet him by saying, "Hey, man, slap me fifty!" By the way, most other kinds of starfish have just five arms.

Hey! There are so many cool creatures with bizarre body parts, we could go on forever giving out these awards. But we have to move on to the next section of the book.

Living upside down in trees comes naturally to the furry three-toed sloth, found in the forests of Central and South America. These unusual animals have large curved claws on their hands and feet that help them grab tree branches extra tightly. Sloths eat, give birth, and sleep with their heads pointing down. Even their body hair is "backwards." It is parted along the belly instead of the back, so rain can easily run off their bodies. When a sloth has to change trees, he crawls on the ground extremely slowly.

Sloth

Spectacled flying fox

Bats have no trouble hanging from their feet, thanks to their special coat-hanger-like claws. In fact, some bat scientists once removed some hibernating bats from their perches, weighed them, and rehooked them without the bats ever waking up. Bats don't feel dizzy when they go topsy-turvy because their circulatory system works in the opposite direction of most creatures. In fact, the only times that bats are *not* upside down are when they're flying, getting rid of body waste, or giving birth.

Blue-crowned hanging parrot

The blue-crowned hanging parrot lives north of Australia on the Malay Peninsula and on islands such as Anamba, Nias, and Belitung. This bizarre bird flips himself head-down when he's sleeping, eating, or playing with other hanging parrots. Zoologists don't know why this parrot hangs. Some experts think he turns over to blend in with the green, leafy trees. Other scientists think these parrots flip over to help them reach their favorite meals of nectar and pollen.

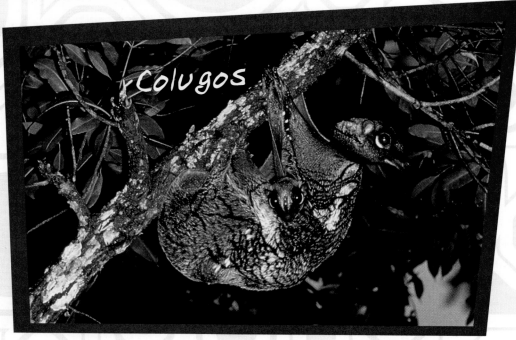

Colugos

In the rain forests of Southeast Asia, colugos dangle upside down from tree branches. They look a little like sloths until they take off into the air and glide gracefully to a nearby tree. To pull off this amazing trapeze act, a colugo uses his parachutelike skin, which stretches across the back of his whole body.

cassiopeia jellyfish

Unlike other jellyfish, the cassiopeia (pronounced "kass-ee-OH-pee-uh") lives in shallow waters of the ocean with her tentacles pointing up toward the surface. This odd position helps this jellyfish get her favorite meal — algae. The algae live on the cassiopeia's tentacles, which make a good home for algae because they get so much sunlight. The cassiopeia can paralyze her prey with a mucous spray, but it is harmless to humans.

Faster Than A Speeding Bullet

Wooow, these guys are hard to keep up with! While we catch our breath, check out these pictures of the speediest creatures in the air, on land, and in the water.

peregrine falcon

When a peregrine falcon swoops down on her prey, you don't want to be in her way. This bird's powerful wings and sleek body shape let her zoom through the air as fast as 200 miles per hour! That's faster than any other creature on earth.

Cheetah

The swiftest human on record ran at a speed of 23 miles per hour. When a cheetah really turns on the juice, he can go about three times faster — 70 miles per hour. It's no surprise they're the fastest animal on land. But remember, this incredible creature wouldn't be able to shift into high gear if he didn't have long legs, a top-notch respiratory system, and a super-flexible backbone!

Sailfish

When a sailfish really gets going, she can speed along at about 65 miles per hour. This fish's powerful, streamlined body can grow up to 12 feet long, from the end of her sleek tail to the tip of her sharp, spearlike bill. She also has a massive, colorful fin on her back that helps her zip through the water. Sometimes, she can build up enough speed to leap high above the water's surface.

¡PEEEE-YEWWW!

Zorilla

When the creatures on these pages need to protect themselves, they create a horrible stink. Lucky for you, this isn't a scratch 'n' sniff book!

Although the zorilla is related to the skunk, his foul-smelling scent is even worse. Zorillas live in Africa. They use their powerful spray to keep lions and other enemies far away from their young and any food they've stashed away. Other creatures can smell the zorilla's stench from over a mile away.

To avoid being eaten, the shieldbug, or stinkbug, gives off a terrible odor that can be sprayed as far as one foot. This smelly defense also helps this animal protect his food by covering it with a bitter taste. The bright spots on this insect's wings warn predators to keep away if they don't want to smell worse than rotten eggs!

shieldbug

Hoatzin

The hoatzin is one foul-smelling fowl. This South American creature, nicknamed the stinkbird, tells other rain forest creatures to keep their distance by creating an awful smell.

Morph Masters

Small, thin animals sometimes make themselves look big and tough to scare off their enemies.

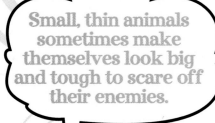

Some of the mighty morphing champs you're about to meet even try to imitate other species. To see how effective this can be, check out these photos!

Bridal burrfish

When the bridal burrfish wants to intimidate her underwater foes, she expands her body into a round ball. All the little thornlike objects on her skin stand out, which makes larger fish think twice about taking a chomp out of her body.

Moth caterpillar

If a Costa Rican moth caterpillar is being pursued by a bird, he will magically turn into a ready-to-strike viper. At least that's what the caterpillar wants the hungry bird to think. What *really* happens during this quick-change act is that the moth caterpillar swivels his body, so his tail is facing his enemy. Since his tail has bold, black marks on each side, it looks like the eyes of a threatening snake.

Although the Indian cobra can deliver a venomous bite, she's still in danger of being attacked from behind. So, to scare off predators such as mongooses, this cobra spreads the upper part of her body to form a hood. As you can see, the black pattern on her skin looks like the face of another, even more frightening animal.

Indian cobra

Frilled lizard

Next Halloween, if you really want to spook your neighbors, dress up as an Australian frilled lizard. When this 18-inch creature wants to make an enemy panic, he ruffles out his neck scales, opens his mouth ferociously, and makes wild hissing noises. Of course, all of this is just show. The frilled lizard's favorite meal is small insects.

Ostriches

You wouldn't think that eight-foot ostriches would be any good at hiding out in the middle of hot, dry plains. But they are! The trick is that they can make themselves look like a clump of round, leafy bushes with thin trunks. To pull off this effect, ostriches tuck down their heads, raise their tails, and fluff out their feathers. If, by some chance, a predator figures out the truth, ostriches have a great means of escape. They can run at about 45 miles per hour!

Armored Animals

For excellent protection from predators, some animals have developed super-thick skin or other types of armor. That way, their soft, gooey insides are hidden behind natural suits of armor.

No wonder you don't move very fast, this shell's heavy!

Leopard tortoise

Armadillo

The armadillo, whose name means "little armored one" in Spanish, lives in South America and the southern part of the United States. She has an awesome way of traveling through thorny woods and escaping from enemies. Since most of her body is covered with thick, hinged plates, she simply curls into a tight ball and rolls away at high speed. For water travel, the armadillo has two choices. She either sinks to the bottom of a river and walks along the bottom, or she swallows enough air so her heavy body floats along the top.

Pangolin

The pangolin's mighty suit of armor is actually made up of thick pieces of keratin, the same stuff found in human hair and nails. Like the armadillo, when the pangolin wants to avoid danger, she curls up into a hard little ball that most predators can't chew through. She even uses her long, scaly tail to lock herself closed. This creature can also ruin a predator's appetite by spraying a smelly liquid at him.

Thorny devil

Normally, an eight-inch lizard would make a great meal for many Australian snakes. But the thorny devil is definitely an exception. His leathery skin is covered with sharp spikes that scare off many of his predators. This leaves the gentle thorny devil free to wander the desert and eat ants.

Saltwater crocodile

The strong and sturdy saltwater crocodile hangs out in the rivers and swamps of the Philippines, New Guinea, and northern Australia. As if a giant set of teeth and powerful jaws weren't enough, his 15–26 foot body is covered with thick, shingled skin that makes him almost impenetrable.